AWAY FROM KEYBOARD

IF YOU LIKE EXPLORING, ADVENTURING OR TEAMWORK GAMES TRY THIS!

by DANIEL **MAULEÓN**

Raintree is an imprint of Capstone Global Library Limited, a company incorporated in England and Wales having its registered office at 264 Banbury Road, Oxford, OX2 7DY – Registered company number: 6695582

www.raintree.co.uk
myorders@raintree.co.uk

Text © Capstone Global Library Limited 2021
The moral rights of the proprietor have been asserted.

All rights reserved. No part of this publication may be reproduced in any form or by any means (including photocopying or storing it in any medium by electronic means and whether or not transiently or incidentally to some other use of this publication) without the written permission of the copyright owner, except in accordance with the provisions of the Copyright, Designs and Patents Act 1988 or under the terms of a licence issued by the Copyright Licensing Agency, Barnard's Inn, 86 Fetter Lane, London, EC4A 1EN (www.cla.co.uk). Applications for the copyright owner's written permission should be addressed to the publisher.

Edited by Anna Butzer
Designed by Kyle Grenz
Original illustrations © Capstone Global Library Limited 2021
Picture research by Tracy Cummins
Production by Tori Abraham
Originated by Capstone Global Library Ltd

978 1 3982 0444 7 (hardback)
978 1 3982 0445 4 (paperback)

British Library Cataloguing in Publication Data
A full catalogue record for this book is available from the British Library.

Acknowledgements
All photographs by Capstone: Karon Dubke; Marcy Morin and Sarah Schuette, Project Production; Heidi Thompson, Art Director
Design elements: Shutterstock

Every effort has been made to contact copyright holders of material reproduced in this book. Any omissions will be rectified in subsequent printings if notice is given to the publisher.

All the internet addresses (URLs) given in this book were valid at the time of going to press. However, due to the dynamic nature of the internet, some addresses may have changed, or sites may have changed or ceased to exist since publication. While the author and publisher regret any inconvenience this may cause readers, no responsibility for any such changes can be accepted by either the author or the publisher.

Printed and bound in India

CONTENTS

ONWARD HO! 4

DEEP SPACE TERRARIUM 6

VEIL OF VINES 8

SWASHBUCKLING SWORD 10

ARMOUR AND HELMET 12

WANDERER'S STAFF 16

ADVENTURER'S SATCHEL 18

CRAFTY COMPASS 20

X MARKS THE SPOT 22

WOODLAND HIDEAWAY 24

ADVENTURE BARS 28

HANDY SCORECARD 30

FIND OUT MORE 32

ONWARD HO!

Exploring and adventuring video games take you to other worlds! You can journey into magical kingdoms, dark dungeons and even the vast reaches of outer space. But when you need to disconnect from the digital world, don't despair! There are countless ways to bring the coolest parts of those games to life in the real world.

Need proof? Well, look no further. This book is jam-packed with projects any digital dungeon crawler will love! From deep space terrariums to swashbuckling swords and satchels, there's no limit to the adventures you're about to have. And all you need are a few craft supplies and a lot of imagination.

So what are you waiting for? It's time to build, explore and discover the world around you. But don't go it alone. Pull a friend into the adventure as well. After all, every quest is even better with a trusty Player Two at your side. Onward ho!

DEEP SPACE TERRARIUM

Does the hair on your arms stand up when you explore alien video game environments? If so, bring that zing to life with your own deep space terrarium. Strange worlds await!

1. Use the marker to draw a large oval shape on one side of the bottle. Ask an adult to cut out the shape with a utility knife.

2. Hot glue the oval shape to the other side of the bottle. This piece will act as a stand so the bottle doesn't roll away.

3. Fill the bottom of the bottle with coloured rocks.

4. Sprinkle the kinetic sand across the rocks in layers so that it falls evenly. Use your thumb to gently press the sand into place. Leave a few rocks exposed.

5. Place your air plants and any other outer space decorations on top of the sand.

YOU WILL NEED:

- marker pen
- 2-litre drinks bottle
- utility knife
- hot glue gun
- small coloured rocks
- kinetic sand
- air plants

VEIL OF VINES

In the video game world, a curtain of vines is a doorway to adventure. Treasure and secret realms almost always lie hidden on the other side. What mysteries will lie behind your own veil of vines?

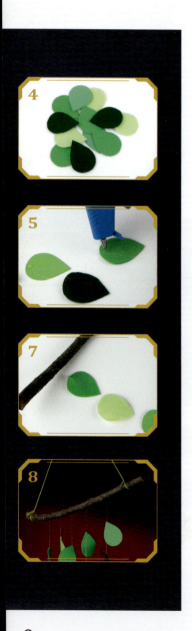

1. Measure the distance from where you want to hang your vine curtain to the floor.

2. Cut a string of fishing line to the length measured in step 1.

3. Tape a large piece of wax paper to a flat surface. Lay a piece of fishing line across it.

4. Cut out 20 to 30 felt and cardstock leaf shapes. Make your leaves similar sizes.

5. Put a dot of hot glue on the back of each leaf and press it onto the fishing line. Continue adding leaves to cover most of the fishing line. Leave about 15 centimetres (6 inches) of fishing line empty at one end.

6. Repeat steps 2 to 5 with additional strings of fishing line.

7. Once you have the desired number of vines, remove the wax paper and tie the leafless ends of the vines to the tree branch.

8. Cut a piece of twine that is slightly longer than the branch. Tie the ends of the twine to the ends of the branch.

9. Place a self-adhesive hook where you want your curtain to hang. Centre the twine over the hook so the curtain hangs straight.

YOU WILL NEED:

- tape measure
- scissors
- fishing line
- sticky tape
- wax paper
- green felt
- green cardstock
- hot glue gun
- tree branch
- twine
- self-adhesive hooks

SWASHBUCKLING SWORD

Whether cutting through wild vines or thwarting menacing monsters, every hero needs a sword. If you don't have one, don't worry! Forge your very own and leap into action!

YOU WILL NEED:

- cardboard
- pencil
- scissors
- hot glue gun
- 4 large craft sticks
- black tape
- gold tape
- silver tape

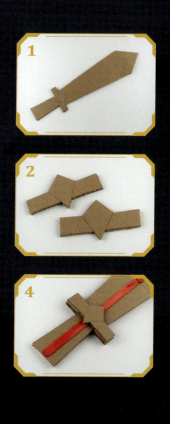

1. Draw a sword shape on cardboard with a pencil. Cut out the sword with scissors.

2. Trace the hilt's shape onto the cardboard twice. Cut out these shapes.

3. Glue four large craft sticks in a line down the middle of your sword and handle. The sticks will help support and strengthen your sword.

4. Sandwich your sword between the two hilt pieces. Glue the pieces in place.

5. Wrap the handle in black tape, including the hilt. Add some gold tape to the hilt to decorate.

6. Wrap the blade in silver tape.

ARMOUR AND HELMET

Now that you have a sword, it's time to gear up for adventure. This body armour and helmet will help you ward off any monsters that cross your path!

YOU WILL NEED:

- cardboard box about the size of your upper body
- utility knife
- large paper plate
- pencil
- silver tape
- silver paint
- black marker
- string
- hot glue gun
- buttons or bottle tops

1. Ask an adult to cut off one short side of the cardboard box with a utility knife. Using the plate as a pattern, draw a circle on the other short side large enough for your head. Cut out the circle.

2. Put the cardboard on over your head like a poncho. Ask a friend to draw lines to mark the waistline and armholes. Take the box off and cut the cardboard at the markings. The box should now look like a vest.

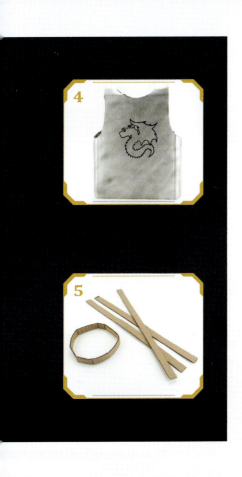

3. Try on the armour vest and bend the sides to adjust it as needed. Use tape to hold the sides together if necessary.

4. Paint the armour silver. Use a marker to add a crest or logo to the front.

5. For the helmet, use a piece of string to measure around your head. With an adult's help, cut four 2.5-cm- (1-inch-) wide strips of cardboard to the measured length. Hot glue the ends of one strip together to make a loop that fits around your head. There should be a little wiggle room.

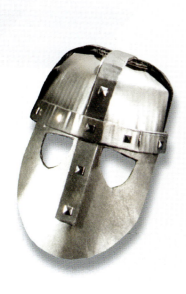

6. Bend another cardboard strip into an upside-down U shape. Glue the shape inside the circle to form the top of the helmet. Repeat with another cardboard strip. Make it cross the first strip at the top centre of the helmet. Trim away the ends that hang down under the edge of the circle.

7. Cut a 7.6-cm- (3-inch-) wide cardboard circle. Glue it under the cross point at the top of the helmet.

8. Cut four triangles with rounded corners to fit inside the open spaces in the frame. Hot glue them to the inside of the frame.

9. Cut a U-shaped piece of cardboard to use as a face shield. Cut smaller U shapes for eyeholes.

10. Hot glue the face shield inside the front of the helmet rim. Glue a strip of 2.5-cm- (1-inch-) wide cardboard between the eyeholes to form a nose guard.

11. Hot glue metal buttons or bottle tops to look like rivets in the helmet frame. Paint the helmet silver and allow it to dry. Now put on your armour and helmet, grab your sword and get ready for battle!

WANDERER'S STAFF

All good explorers need a wanderer's staff to help them on their adventures. This staff even lights up to show the way on the darkest of paths.

YOU WILL NEED:

- long, sturdy stick
- penknife
- paint
- paintbrush
- leather cording
- beads
- small compass
- 2-litre drinks bottle
- marker
- utility knife
- hot glue gun
- battery-powered light

1. Find a long, sturdy stick. Ask an adult to strip off any bark with the penknife.

2. Paint the stick to decorate it any way you like.

3. Wrap leather cording around the top of the stick to create a grip. Attach beads or a small compass to the leather cording if you like.

4. Draw a large geometric shape on the side of the plastic bottle with a marker. Ask an adult to cut out this shape with a utility knife.

5. Fold the plastic shape in half three or four times. Press the creases firmly.

6. Unfold the plastic shape and trace the creases with the marker. This is your crystal.

7. Glue the crystal to the top of the stick.

8. Turn on the battery-powered light. Glue it inside the crystal.

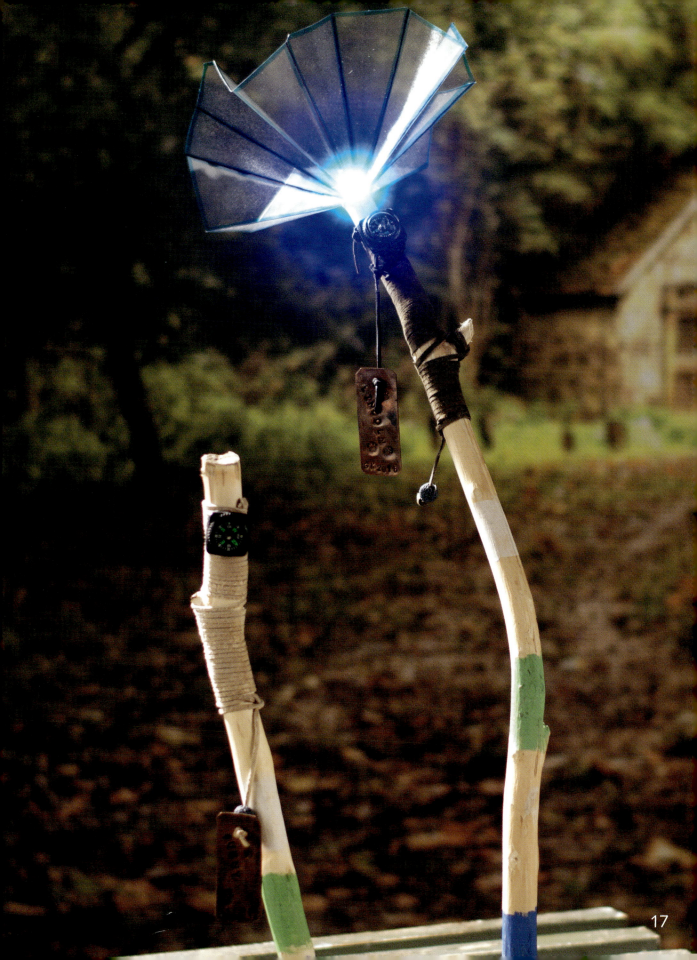

ADVENTURER'S SATCHEL

With a wanderer's staff in hand, you're going to need something to carry the rest of your adventuring gear. Luckily, this do-it-yourself adventurer's satchel will keep all your tools close at hand.

YOU WILL NEED:

- old insulated lunch bag
- cleaning cloth
- carabiner
- brown tape
- green tape
- resealable sandwich bag
- scissors

1. Wipe out the inside and outside of the lunch bag with a damp cloth and allow it to dry.

2. Attach the carabiner to the back of the lunch bag with a 5-cm (2-inch) piece of brown tape. Make sure that the part of the carabiner that opens faces outwards.

3. Wrap the body of the lunch bag in brown tape. Make sure you pass at least one strip through the carabiner to help keep it connected. Be careful not to cover any fasteners used to keep the lunch bag closed.

4. Attach a loop of tape to the back of the resealable plastic bag. Stick the bag to the lunch bag's flap.

5. Cover the lunch bag's flap in green tape. Wrap around the sides of the resealable bag, but leave the top free to open and close.

6. Cut a 91-cm-(3-foot-) long piece of brown tape. Carefully fold it lengthways into a 2.5-cm-(1-inch-) wide strip. Use a small piece of tape to connect the ends of the strip together to make a loop.

7. Put the loop over your body so it hangs diagonally from your left shoulder to your right hip.

8. Attach the bag to the shoulder strap with the carabiner.

9. Pack the adventure bag with any supplies you need for your journey. It should fit a small torch, a water bottle and light rain poncho. Use the resealable bag to store trail mix or other snacks.

CRAFTY COMPASS

In the thick of an adventure, it's easy to lose your way. But you don't need to get lost if you get crafty. Just build a compass to help point you in the right direction.

1. Use the scissors to cut a 9-cm-(3.5-inch-) long piece of wool. Tie one end of the wool around the o-ring.

2. Stretch the o-ring carefully to place the button magnet inside it.

3. Wrap red tape around one screw and white tape around the other screw.

4. Place the red screw on one side of the button magnet and the white screw on the other side to make the compass needle.

5. Ask an adult to cut the dome top off the 2-litre bottle with a utility knife.

6. Trace the base of the dome on the cardstock with a marker. Cut out the circle with scissors.

7. Label north, south, east and west around the circle. Hot glue the circle to the base of the dome to create the compass casing.

8. Unscrew the bottle lid and hot glue the free end of the wool to the inside of the lid. Once dry, carefully slide the compass needle into the dome.

9. Tighten and adjust the lid until the compass needle aligns with the labels for north and south.

X MARKS THE SPOT

Do you love the rush of unearthing hidden treasure in an adventure game? Capture that feeling in the real world with hidden treasures that bring "X marks the spot" to life!

YOU WILL NEED:

- scissors
- gold tape
- plastic container with lid
- black tape
- 10 wooden coins
- markers
- small notebook
- 2 short pencils

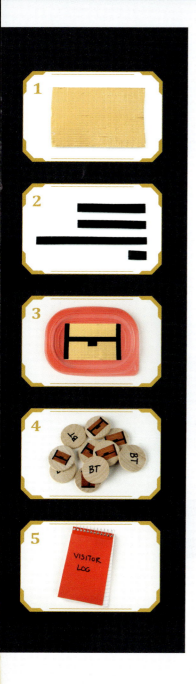

1. Cut an 8-cm-(3-inch-) long piece of gold tape.
2. Cut thin strips of black tape in various lengths.
3. Arrange the black strips of tape on the gold tape to create a treasure box on the lid of the plastic container. Trim off any extra black tape.
4. Use markers to draw treasure boxes on one side of the wooden coins. Write your initials on the other side of the wooden coins.
5. Write "Visitor Log" on the cover of the notebook.
6. Make two columns on the first page of the notebook. Label one column "First Name" and the other column "Adventurer Notes".
7. Place the wooden coins, visitor log and short pencils inside the treasure box container.
8. Hide the treasure box in your house or garden.
9. Think of clues for finding the treasure box. Write them down on scraps of paper.
10. Invite your friends over. One at a time, challenge them to find the treasure box using your clues. Ask each friend to take one wooden coin and write a note in the visitor log when they find the box.

LEVEL UP!

Make 10 treasure boxes and hide them in a local park. Create clues for finding each one. Then challenge your friends to find them all. The person who finds all 10 boxes the fastest wins!

WOODLAND HIDEAWAY

Every adventurer needs a place to relax after a hard day of exploring. Just gather some sticks, branches and a few simple materials to build the perfect woodland hideaway.

YOU WILL NEED:

- 2 short, pointed sticks
- 1 m (3 feet) of string
- 6 flexible branches, 2.5 cm (1 inch) thick by 2 m (6 feet) long
- large leaves or long grass
- 12 sturdy branches, 60 cm to 1 m (2 to 3 feet) long
- several thin branches
- thin, strong wire

1. Find a level patch of ground 1.8 to 2.4 m (6 to 8 feet) wide. Clear it of rocks and sticks. Tie one short, pointed stick to the end of the string. Push the stick into the ground at the centre of the hut's location.

2. Tie the second pointed stick to the other end of the string. Use the stick to scrape a 2-m- (6-foot-) wide circle in the ground around the centre stick.

3. Push the thick end of one long branch 15 cm (6 inches) into the ground at the edge of the circle. If the ground is too hard, dig a small hole and place the branch into it. Then fill it with soil and stomp it tightly around the branch.

4. Place a second long branch into the ground directly opposite the first branch.

5. Bend the two long branches towards each other. Overlap the ends by several centimetres and tie them together with wire to form an arch shape.

6. Repeat steps 3 to 5 until the circle is divided into six equal parts. Tie all the arches together at the top to make a dome-shaped frame.

7. Find six sturdy branches about as long as the distance between the ribs of the dome. Use wire to tie each of these branches between the ribs about 60 cm (2 feet) above the ground.

8. Repeat step 7 and tie more branches about 1.2 m (4 feet) above the ground. The frame of your hut should now be solid and stable.

TIPS AND TRICKS!

Wire can be sharp to work with. Make sure you wear gloves to protect your hands. A pair of pliers can also come in handy for twisting the ends of wire together.

9 Make sure you leave a space for a door that you can crawl through. Once the hut is stable, you may need to move a stick up to make the door higher.

10 Gather several long, leafy branches. Work around the hut frame, weaving the leafy branches in and out vertically between the ribs.

11 Finally, weave more leafy branches horizontally through the vertical branches. Then crawl inside and enjoy your cool, shady hideout!

LEVEL UP!

If you have lots of clay soil nearby, you can turn this into a clay hut. Mix clay with water until it's pasty. Plaster the clay all over the leaves inside and out to form a solid dome. Then allow it to dry.

ADVENTURE BARS

Adventures often take you further than you'd expect and can leave you with an empty stomach. Whip up these no-bake granola bars to keep you going!

YOU WILL NEED:

INGREDIENTS
- 312 g (2 cups) oats
- 240 g (1 cup) peanut butter
- 120 ml (½ cup) honey
- 88 g (½ cup) chocolate chips
- 75 g (½ cup) raisins
- 30 g (¼ cup) nuts (optional)

EQUIPMENT
- mixing bowl
- wooden spoon
- 23-cm x 28-cm (9-inch x 11-inch) baking tin
- knife
- clingfilm

1. Mix peanut butter and honey in a bowl. Add in other ingredients and mix well.
2. Pour the mixture into the baking tin. Press the mixture flat and even across the tin.
3. Place the tin in the fridge for one hour.
4. Ask an adult to use a knife to cut the mixture into about 20 bars.
5. Wrap each bar in clingfilm and store in the fridge.

HANDY SCORECARD

When you've finished exploring and adventuring, challenge your friends to a game or two. And don't worry about keeping score. This handy scorecard has you covered!

YOU WILL NEED:

- cardboard
- 2 colours of tape
- clear packing tape
- 2 wooden clothes pegs
- ruler
- scissors
- markers

1. Cut a piece of cardboard into two long, identical rectangles.
2. Use a marker to make three long columns on one piece of cardboard.
3. In the centre column, write the numbers 1 to 10.
4. Cover the left column with one colour of tape. Cover the right column with a different colour tape.
5. Draw a line all the way across the columns under each number.
6. Tape the second piece of cardboard to the back of the first one. Stand the cardboard up so the two pieces form a triangle.
7. Colour the clothes pegs the same colours as the tape you used on the scoreboard.
8. Attach the pegs to the scoreboard to help keep track of the score during a game.

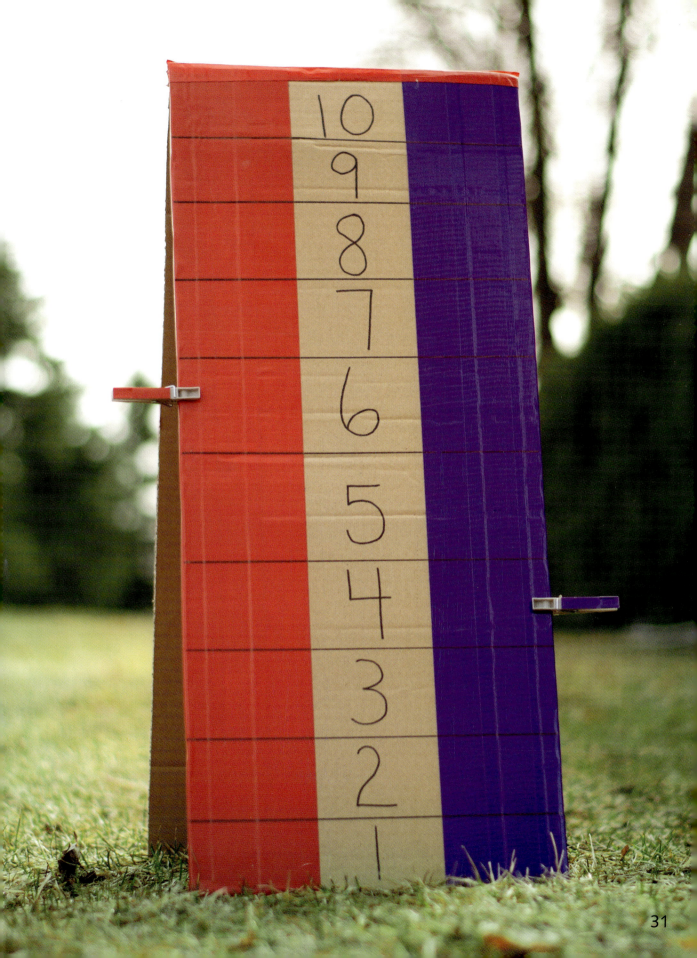

FIND OUT MORE

BOOKS

365 Things to Make and Do (Usborne Activities), Fiona Watt (Usborne, 2007)

Building Projects for Beginners (Hands-On Projects for Beginners), Tammy Enz (Raintree, 2018)

Out of the Box: 25 Incredible Craft Projects You Can Make From Cardboard, Jemma Westing (DK Children, 2017)

WEBSITES

www.bbc.co.uk/cbeebies/curations/the-lets-go-club-craft-activities

www.tate.org.uk/kids/make